Conversations with
Adam and Natasha

CONVERSATIONS WITH ADAM AND NATASHA

BY
R. D. LAING

PANTHEON BOOKS, NEW YORK

Library of Congress Cataloging in Publication Data

Laing, Ronald David.
Conversations with Adam and Natasha.

1. Child psychology—Case studies. I. Laing,
Adam. II. Laing, Natasha. III. Title.
BF721.L27   155.4′092′6   77-5185
ISBN 0-394-42008-X

Manufactured in the United States of America

FIRST EDITION

Introduction

The conversations in this anthology were written down over a six-year period as part of a journal I keep. They are all recorded from memory. No tape recorder ever was used. Nearly all were committed to paper within twenty-four hours of occurrence.

None of them was structured or set up. They are without exception part of the flux of uncontrived happenings in the course of my family life. The children are in the habit of seeing me jot things down; a lot of my writing is done here or there, often with other people, including children, around. I do not think that the fact of writing them down has significantly affected their character.

I have always enjoyed dialogue and reciprocity generally, with and without words. However, I have spent a considerable part of my life studying unenjoyable communication, miscommunication, and failure to communicate, much of it in family contexts, and in depicting, describing and theorizing about this domain of misery. I have done so largely because I attribute such importance to the way we get on, or not, with the people we live with. It affects everything, our intellectual, spiritual and physical lives as well as our emotional and social.

Those who have studied painful interactions have documented many ways in which we may do one another in, not always knowing we are doing so, or being so done to. Many nuances of ways we may confuse, deceive and hurt ourselves and others, often without realizing it, have been described by the experts in this division of hell in recent years.

However, the other side of the story has not been looked at nearly so much. The language of the happy dialogue of intelligent beings has evolved to an amazing degree of intricacy and complexity. When this dialogue is not knotted, entangled and entangling, then instead of being a deadening, suffocating zone, it is the free and open space between us where we can play with being together, where we question and answer, inquire into what is the case and what is not, for the sheer heaven of it. The patterns of reciprocity which are spun out of this activity synchronously and diachronically are most succinctly epitomized for me, in music, through counterpoint; in visual terms, in the *interlace*.

It is therefore a great pleasure and relief for me to present these dialogues which express so much light-hearted and serious delight; not that they are not sometimes fierce and savage, not that the dark side of things is missing, but that it seems to me, so far, hatred, spite, revenge, jealousy, malice and envy, and the other blights on life, are not seen here triumphant.

In the following pages, we are able to observe the emotional and cognitive development of two children with unimpaired faculties unfolding within the interlace and interweave of relations with adults whom they do not fear and whom they like as they are liked.

After pondering it over a lot, I have decided not to introduce their conversations with a theoretical essay, nor to footnote them in the many places where I have felt tempted to do so. The best order, I think, is to let them stand on their own, and for them to be read, in the first place, with the fewest possible theoretical presuppositions. Such theoretical considerations as are raised by them in many relevant fields—psychoanalysis, developmental epistemology, communications theory, anthropology—can be taken up later. In the meantime, I hope the professionals will find them useful. Yes, so many constructions can be placed on them! In these pages I shall not talk across or over them with my adult voice. Since this book is almost entirely taken up with the voices of children, I expect it may be read as much by children as by adults, and since it needs no professional or scientific expertise, that it will be read as readily by anyone as by adult child specialists.

I hope that these pages will contribute to making apparent that it is just as useful for adults to be in touch with childhood as for children to be in touch with adults. We learn about children only from children. Our understanding of ourselves is enormously impoverished if we are out of touch with childhood. Adults can suffer as much from the deprivation of children in their lives as the other way round. I suspect that children play as important a part in adult "growth and development" as we adults do in theirs. But I don't spend time with them because I have to or because I should or because it is "useful," but simply because I want to.

Having studied human communication for many years now, professionally, I am very aware of what is left out in this book. There are very few indications of the tempo, rhythm, pitch, volume and timbre of the words on the page, and hardly anything about the movements, expressions and gestures which are an inextricable part of the interactional dance.

These conversations emerge out of the time before spoken speech. Both Adam and Natasha enjoyed and enjoy, with no break of continuity, a most intimate reciprocity with their mother, Jutta. The later reciprocal talking of these pages is a form of exchange which emerges out of reciprocities already there.

Indeed, such was the richness of their earlier epoch, before the onslaught of language, that our pleasure in having our children to talk to us was tinged with sadness and nostalgia for the subtlety of their music and dance before they spoke. It's sometimes difficult to keep up with one's children: not to mourn, in gaining a girl, a boy, the loss of a baby and an infant. And by the time this book is being read, the children depicted in its pages will already have grown out of their clothes several times.

Some of these conversations have struck some people as so incredible that I've been asked if I made them up. No, I did not. I could not. However much I would like to lay claim to their invention, I can vouch only for the fact that I have added nothing. I am responsible for deletions and, I suppose inevitably, for some inadvertent omissions. But I have made no additions, no embellishments. I have selected. There are intimacies within family life which I am old-fashioned enough to believe it is unseemly to reveal in public. Indeed, I have hesitated for several years before coming to feel that it does not offend my sense of propriety to disclose this much of a very private domain. This is done with the full accord of my wife—and of the children.

Need I say also that the children have not spent their lives having conversations with me. Their relation to their mother, my wife, is only glimpsed in these pages, but that should be enough to reveal the supreme importance she has in this family's scheme of things.

Nevertheless, with those and other limitations, as far as I know, no similar anthology of dialogues with children has been published.

London, June 1977   R. D. LAING

ADAM   born September 1967

NATASHA   born April 1970

MAX   born June 1975

Conversations with
Adam and Natasha

1

LONDON   *March 1970*

ADAM   have you a long pole?
DADDY   no sorry
ADAM   or a ladder?
DADDY   what do you want it for?
ADAM   I want to knock down the sun and
          break it in two and give mummy it to
          cook and we'll eat it
DADDY   but what will we do without the sun
          in the sky?
ADAM   I don't like it
DADDY   what's wrong with it?
ADAM   it's *boring*
DADDY   but the sun. I'm fond of the sun
ADAM   I'll get another
DADDY   how?
ADAM   I'll buy one
DADDY   where?
ADAM   in Woolworth's
DADDY   I'm glad I haven't got a ladder to reach
          the sun if that's what you would do with it
ADAM   O *daddy* (*pause*)
          haven't you got one I could stand on
          tiptoe on top of, and poke it out with
          a stick?

2

ADAM (*on hearing of fighting, shooting, and killing
        in Kandy, fourteen miles away*)
        I want to go to Kandy and kill people
        and cut them up and eat them for
        breakfast with a big steel gun and a
        stiff trigger
DADDY   why?
ADAM   because I want to shoot a lot of
        people and kill them so they'll be
        dead. Like I did last time
DADDY   how do you mean last time?
ADAM   last time I was here
DADDY   here?
ADAM   last time I was alive
DADDY   how do you know?
ADAM   I remember. I was a soldier. I
        killed a lot of people
DADDY   really
ADAM   did you kill a lot of people last
        time daddy?
DADDY   I don't think so
ADAM   not recently?
DADDY   no
ADAM   but did you kill a lot of people a
        long, long time ago?
DADDY   I may have but I can't remember
ADAM   you can't remember! (*incredulously*)
DADDY   no
ADAM   oh

3

After a storm

ADAM   what's the decoration on the moon?
                  (*before I could answer*)
                  it's a man with a hammer. When it's a storm,
                  that's when he's angry

4

LONDON   *February 1973*

I'm sitting in my armchair reading

Natasha walks in, stifling her sobs, clambers on my lap, positions herself upright, facing away, tilts her head fully back, and bursts into howls and howls and howls.

I make a move to cuddle her but she elbows my arms away, and when I tentatively touch the tips of her fingers by way of some gesture of consolation, she snatches them away, and her howls threaten to turn into shrieks, or even screeches. As her howls continue I have just time to check my impulse to ask her what's the matter, to hug her, stroke her, or offer words of comfort, before, as she is lowering her head and turning to look at me for the first time, her last howl fades. In one smile she says hello, bye-bye, perhaps, thanks daddy. With a sigh of completion, she gets down from my lap, and without a word between us since she came in and without looking back, she ambles out of the door, ready for her next adventure.

5

Before dinner

Natasha is holding her head and howling. Is it bleeding?
Does it need a stitch? No. Nothing serious.
Adam did it with his rifle, she says.

He denies it. Then says he didn't mean it. That means he did. I take
his rifle and guns away from him, and put them up on the top of a
high shelf next to the ceiling.

At dinner

He is going to pour a bucket of water over me when I am asleep in
bed.

He is going to phone the police because I have been nasty to him
and he knows their number.
He'll make a ladder and get his guns down.

And Natasha joins in, on *his* side.
She is going to cut my head off
and then cut my nose off
and

        "I'll have a secret place and
        you won't be able to find me"

After dinner

Adam has found a way to get his rifle and guns down.
He comes into my room with his rifle
        "I'm going to put it where I (*sic*)
        can't find it"
He puts it away

A little later he comes in with it again to show me

ADAM	You might not believe me
ME	Oh I believe you. It's alright
ADAM	No. You just might not believe me.
	I'll just show you

He goes off with the rifle again, to hide it once more where he can't find it. In a few minutes he's back with the rifle, showing me it, almost pedagogically, to make trebly sure I believe it. He goes off. A little later he's back, dressed in a green commando suit, with tin hat and rifle.

ADAM	Order me about
ME	I'm trying to get some work done do you
	mind
ADAM	aw come on order me about

I order him about

Attention. Quick march. Halt. Stand at ease. Shoulder arms. Quick march . . .

.   .   .

It is hours later. Past their bedtime.
Adam and Natasha are drawing. Peace and Quiet
He has borrowed from me my tin of special pens, pencils, felt tips, and nibs

Ah! Now he's just spilled the lot over the
floor!
Arrggh

6

The Grand Old Man bends a long way down, out of politeness (so that his eyes are level with Natasha's), and enquires, with kindly solemnity

	Do you like being you?
NATASHA	yes I like being me. I'm a very nice girl, and a very intelligent girl, and everyone likes me. Even mummy likes me.

7

NATASHA	Daddy. Would you like Mummy to be your mummy?

8

ADAM	What are you reading?
ME	love poems
ADAM	Haven't you any hate poems?
ME	I'm just trying to read these just now if you don't mind
ADAM	(*with glee*) Why don't you write some *hate* poems?

9

Jutta, Adam, and Natasha are off to Stuttgart tomorrow to stay with
Jutta's parents for a week

Bedtime

DADDY	I'm sad you're going away Natasha
NATASHA	I'm not sad today, I'll be sad tomorrow

10

July 1973

Jutta and I haven't been getting on very well recently.
Natasha has become interested in glue, and sellotape: in cutting
things up and sticking them together.
Just now she has been dashing from one wall of my room to the
other, thudding against them

RONNIE	What are you doing?
NATASHA	the heart
RONNIE	the heart?
NATASHA	yes (*she continues thudding against the walls*)
RONNIE	and what does the heart do?
NATASHA	the heart loves (*she stops dashing and thudding*)
RONNIE	the heart loves?
NATASHA	yes
RONNIE	who? what?
NATASHA	the one heart loves many people
RONNIE	the one heart loves many?
NATASHA	the one heart loves many many

ADAM	and how would you like it if—come on daddy, it's your turn
DADDY	if someone shoved spaghetti up your nose
ADAM	and how would you like it if someone mixed up sand and water into some sort of cement and put it down your throat?
DADDY	and how would you like it if someone put you in a large tub—as large as this room—of treacle?
ADAM	and how would you like it if I cut off your nose?
DADDY	and how would you like it if I cut off your arms, and body, and legs, and head—where would you be then?
ADAM	there (*patting me there*) in my body

and how would *you* like it if I cut your body into teeny weeny bits (*illustrating with right thumb and forefinger*) and cut these little bits into little bits?

DADDY	(*split second's hesitation*)
ADAM	(*before I can get my breath*) where would you be then?
DADDY	(*he's got me on the run*)
ADAM	(*pressing home his advance*) you tell me
DADDY	I don't know
ADAM	(*flash*)*

* With both arms, and whole body: like a conductor indicating a split-second flash of silence.

DADDY	I might be like space
ADAM	(*flash*)
DADDY	or I might be finished
ADAM	(*flash*)
DADDY	what do you think?
ADAM	(*flash*)
DADDY	do you remember?
ADAM	(*flash*)
DADDY	do you know?
ADAM	(*flash*)
DADDY	maybe finished
ADAM	mmmm

12

October 1973

Natasha is bashing at a door with a shoe

NATASHA	I want to kill a little thing, daddy
DADDY	Oh. That's not very nice
	How would you like it if someone
	wanted to kill you?
NATASHA	I want to kill it
	I want to kill it
	I want to kill it
	and that will be the end of it

13

Adam has been trying to wriggle out of something

JUTTA   you can't cheat me
              I'm smarter than you
              I can *see* and smell your farts!

14

November 1973

Evening

Jutta and I have had a quarrel, and she has gone to a party alone.

I am sitting, writing, in a bad mood.
Natasha comes into the room, and starts to fiddle with sellotape.
She crumples a length of it, and spirals it around.

DADDY   what are you doing?
NATASHA   I want to make a sword
DADDY   (*testily*) You can't make a sword out of sellotape

I was annoyed she hadn't confirmed my theory that it was an umbilical cord. Still.

She takes two pieces of white paper, and folds each exactly alike.

NATASHA   this is mummy piece
              and this is daddy piece

She sellotapes them together and puts them on my desk

NATASHA   This is for *both* of you
DADDY   thank you, Natasha

She takes four pieces of paper and the sellotape: goes away and comes back in a few minutes.

She has folded and sellotaped two sets of two pieces

NATASHA   This one's for you (*giving it to me*),
           and this one's for mummy (*taking it with her
           to her room*)

Later the same evening

Adam, Natasha, and I have been flying paper airplanes.
Now it's quiet. Adam is watching TV in the children's room

Natasha is sitting reflectively in my armchair
I am sitting at my desk nearby

NATASHA   Daddy?
DADDY   yes Natasha
NATASHA   maybe mummy'll be *serious* when she comes
           home
DADDY   how do you mean?
NATASHA   maybe she'll be serious
DADDY   about what?
NATASHA   maybe she'll *scream*. (*pause*) At Adam.

15

Natasha and I are throwing paper airplanes back and forth to each other.
When it goes straight to her, and she fails to catch it she cries

> You missed me

and when it goes wide of me, and I fail to catch it she cries

> You missed it

16

Natasha wants sellotape for Xmas

17

December 1973

Adam is allowed, on his own, to play with a match box, to take matches out of the box, and to strike matches.

Natasha is allowed, on her own, to play with a match box, to take matches out, but not to strike them.
Just now, she can, because I'm around.

NATASHA   (*striking matches, blowing them out, and musing, disconsolately*)
Striking is better than taking out
(*then, brightening up*)
but I can *leave** more than Adam

18

December 1973

I'm sitting writing
Scraps have been occurring to me.

ME   I can't even see
why a flea is so wee
I can't even see
da da dum da da dee
let alone where I'll be
         when I die
(*talking to myself*)
Where shall I be when I die? (*pause*) I don't know
NATASHA   (*rather primly, as though I should know better*)
nor do I. Nor does anyone know that

* That is, on her plate.

19

JUTTA   The Emperor had the most beautiful palace
in all the world so that all the people passing
by would be sure to notice it

NATASHA   I can't breathe

JUTTA   I won't read anymore if you go on like that

NATASHA   I'm holding my breath

JUTTA   I'm finished. Put out the light

NATASHA   I want it on

JUTTA   put it out

NATASHA   I want it on

JUTTA   I'm not going to tell you a million times

NATASHA   a million hurts me

20

1973

Natasha is holding onto one of my legs as I am standing lighting my pipe. I'm frightened some lighted ash or sparks will fall on her.

ME   you shouldn't hold onto my leg when I'm
lighting my pipe or you'll burn yourself

NATASHA   you shouldn't hold onto someone's leg when
you're lighting your pipe or you'll burn
yourself

21

DADDY   why did the peacock scream?
ADAM   because he couldn't see himself
NATASHA because he wanted to hear himself

22

January 1974

ME   don't do that
ADAM   I will if you won't let me

23

January 1974

KIRA   Adam is following me
ME   why are you following her?
ADAM   I follow her
        'cos she follows me

24

Natasha and Adam are very fond of smarties these days.
They come to me for them. I give them more than Jutta thinks is
good for them.

NATASHA   (*to Jutta*) I love daddy because he buys me
                   smarties
DADDY   (*somewhat hurt*) is that why you love daddy?
NATASHA   yes that's why I love you

A few days later

NATASHA   have you any smarties?
DADDY   yes (*and gives her some*)
NATASHA   and for Adam?
DADDY   I've got some for him too

She goes away with them, and comes back after she has eaten them.

NATASHA   I love you daddy. I don't just love
                   you because you bring me smarties.
                   It's not just because you bring me
                   smarties

25

Afternoon

Natasha is hitting a wicker chair with a wooden hatchet made by Adam this afternoon

DADDY   ok that's enough (*it goes on*) that's
                    enough (*it goes on*) stop it (*she
                    continues*) I'll take the hatchet away
                    (*even harder bangs*) I'll take the hatchet
                    away and put you out of the room
NATASHA   I'll hit you in the eye first
DADDY   ok

I wrest the hatchet out of her grip and seize her wrist. I'm prepared to drag her out of the room. But she's already walking out herself and just as I get to the door to slam it on her, she slams it right on my face, flinging back at me as she marches off

        Now you're locked in For Ever and Ever

Evening

It's been somewhat hectic. A boxing match with Adam. A tickling session with both of them. It's quiet again, though I'm feeling a bit frayed, like that wool lying around they've been using to tie onto chair and table legs to stretch across the floor in the hope of tripping people up. I gather it up, slump on a chair, and, absently, wind it

NATASHA   what do you think *you're* doing
ME   I'm winding up some wool
NATASHA   you're winding up your*self, that's* what you're
                    doing. You're winding up your*self* that's what
                    I think you're doing

ADAM	what do shells do?
DADDY	they're like bombs. They explode and destroy. That's all.
ADAM	but you can take the detonator out
DADDY	er, yes—you can. And if they can't explode anymore they can become an ornament. Like this.

This, is three shells (a larger one, standing upright, and two smaller ones) arranged together as a crucifix with the figure of Christ Crucified on the cross they form. I have it on my mantelpiece

DADDY	You can do that with them
ADAM	what's that?
DADDY	it's a man being crucified
ADAM	what's "crucified"?
DADDY	they used to make a large cross out of tree trunks, stick it in the ground, and nail someone on it like that till they died
ADAM	why did they do that to people?
DADDY	to punish people. They don't do that now
ADAM	I know. They put them in jail or treat them

27

23 January 1974

NATASHA   (*listening to the clavichord*) That's beautiful.
               That's very difficult, I can *easily* do
               very difficult things by practicing

28

                                              February 1974

DADDY   what was the first thing you saw when you came
               out of mummy's tummy?
NATASHA   mummy's pussa, that's the first thing I saw when
               I came out of mummy's tummy
DADDY   and what was mummy's pussa like?
NATASHA   mummy's pussa was like mummy's secret heart,
               that's what mummy's pussa was like
DADDY   and what was mummy's secret heart like?
NATASHA   mummy's secret heart was like your two eyes,
               that's what mummy's secret heart was like
DADDY   and what are my two eyes like?
NATASHA   your two eyes are like your nose, that's what
               your two eyes are like
DADDY   and what is my nose like?
NATASHA   your nose is like your teeth, that's what your
               nose is like
DADDY   and what are my teeth like?
NATASHA   your teeth are like your toes, that's what
               your teeth are like
DADDY   and what are my toes like?
NATASHA   your toes are like your fingers, that's what
               your toes are like
DADDY   and what are my fingers like?

NATASHA	your fingers are like your throat,
	that's what your fingers are like
DADDY	and what is my throat like?
NATASHA	your throat is like between your knees,
	that's what your throat is like
DADDY	and what is between my knees like?
NATASHA	between your knees is like between
	your eyes, that's what between your knees
	is like
DADDY	and what is between my eyes like?
NATASHA	between your eyes is like your next head,
	that's what between your eyes is like
DADDY	and what is my next head like?
NATASHA	don't be silly

29

DADDY	Natasha. I have to go away for a little while
NATASHA	can I come with you?
DADDY	no I have to go away by myself for a little while
NATASHA	and you're coming back in a little while?
DADDY	yes
NATASHA	alright daddy (*reflective silence*) but daddy?
DADDY	yes Natasha
NATASHA	do you love me daddy?
DADDY	yes I do love you Natasha
NATASHA	well if you love me you have to let me be near you you have to let me be near you if you love me

30

OLD GENTLEMAN	what can Natasha do?
NATASHA	I can blow up *most* balloons myself

31

NATASHA   here is a present for you and Jutta
           it's for both of you
           it's a ball of wire
           I found the wire in the garden and I
           thought I would like to give you and
           Jutta a present so I made it into a ball
           it didn't take long
           you can play with it if you like
           you can throw it to each other if you like
           I don't mind if it falls,
           if it's an accident
           and I don't mind if it breaks,
           if it's an accident
           it's alright
           I'll fix it it won't take long
ME   thank you Natasha
           I'll put it here on my desk
NATASHA   yes you must take care of it
           you can throw it to each other
           it's for *both* of you

32

Two days ago

ADAM   when do we go back to school
JUTTA   the day after tomorrow
ADAM   when is that?
NATASHA   two sleeps

33

30 April 1974

Natasha is playing with Natasha

NATASHA   (*to herself*)
(*fast*)
(*pointing to her nose*)   this is my foot
(*pointing to her eyes*)   this is my nose
(*pointing to her foot*)   this is my eyes
(*pointing to her mouth*)   this is my neck
(*pointing to her bottom*)   this is my head
(*pointing to her ankle*)   this is my wrist
(*pause*)
(*faster*)
my face is my tummy
my tummy's my eyes
my eyes are my tongue
my tongue is my ankles
my ankles are my hands
(*pause*)
cross your hands
cross your legs
cross your eyes
cross your nose
(*gurgles of amusement*)

34

My study

NATASHA   (*with abrupt unsolicited finality*)
           there's no monster in *this* room
DADDY   Oh
NATASHA   No. I looked under the mat (*conclusively*)
DADDY   How could a monster be under the mat?

She looks at me as though I don't know *anything*

35

NATASHA I don't need a night-light anymore daddy
      I'm not afraid of the dark anymore
      'cos I don't see pictures anymore
DADDY   a night-light's still nice though
      you don't have to be afraid to have
      one
NATASHA No. But I don't see pictures anymore

36

NATASHA	are you sad?
JUTTA	yes
NATASHA	are you sad about life?
JUTTA	yes
NATASHA	I still like you (*pause*)
	shall I be your mummy?
JUTTA	O Natasha
NATASHA	I'll be your mummy and you can have
	a rest for a little while, alright?
JUTTA	alright
NATASHA	alright

She gives Jutta a big hug and a kiss and runs off. She returns after a few minutes

	I don't want to be your mummy anymore
	Was that nice?
JUTTA	yes. Thank you Natasha
NATASHA	that's alright.
	You a little less sad now?
JUTTA	yes

37

Jutta is crying and moaning in bed

NATASHA	why are you crying mummy?
JUTTA	I don't know
NATASHA	are you crying about life?
JUTTA	yes (*pause, sobs*)
NATASHA	we're not going to die
JUTTA	we'll all have to die sooner or later
NATASHA	but we're not going to die *soon*
	we're not going to die till later.
	We'll die *later* (*comfortingly*)

38

31 July 1974

Dinner

I pour out meticulously, *exactly* the same amount of fruit juice for
both Adam and Natasha

NATASHA   I've got more than Adam

Jutta serves Natasha as far as humanly possible the same size help-
ing as Adam's

NATASHA   I've got more than Adam. Mine is more
               than Adam's
ADAM   No it isn't
NATASHA   yes it is (*tears*)

She ate hardly anything, and immediately when Adam had finished
his plate, almost as fast as me, she announced, triumphantly

NATASHA   I've *left* more than Adam

39

Ever since Natasha has been putting her shoes on herself (for more than a year now), she has almost always put them on the "wrong" feet.

It could not have been a random error.

A year ago, for two or three months, she *always* put them on the wrong feet: and refused to change them. This used to bother Jutta who would *insist* she change them before going out, and predicted dire consequences to her feet, and to her, if she didn't.

In the last few months she has been coming into my room in the mornings and asking

"Is it right?"

Occasionally it is, but usually it isn't

Last week is the first week ever that they have been "right" every time.

40

August 1974

Bedtime. Tuck in. Say your prayers

ADAM	Ronnie?
RONNIE	yes
ADAM	is it alright if I say "God bless God"?
RONNIE	. . . er, yyyes, I suppose so
ADAM	what does it mean?
RONNIE	I've no idea what it means
ADAM	is it alright?
RONNIE	yes it's alright
ADAM	goodnight Ronnie
RONNIE	goodnight Adam

41

ADAM I'm frightened

ME of what?

ADAM I said something, I don't know whether it's alright

ME what did you say?

ADAM do you know the marriage ceremony?

ME yes

ADAM I said a bit of it

ME what bit?

ADAM I now pronounce you man and wife

ME who did you say it to?

ADAM a doll

ME what doll?

ADAM Natasha's little Japanese doll

ME Natasha's little Japanese doll

ADAM will it be alright?

ME yes it'll be alright

42

ME	. . . and happy dreams, and don't forget your prayers
NATASHA	and don't forget *your* prayers
ME	God bless . . .
NATASHA	(*interrupting*)
	God bless nothing. God bless nothing.
	God bless NOTHING
ADAM	God bless God

43

20 October 1974

Natasha often asks me to do up her shoe or boot laces. A few weeks ago I was doing them several times a day. She specifies which foot first, what pattern, how firm, the type of knot, and the size of bow. It all has to be precisely symmetrical.

Until the last two weeks it always had to be a double knot. But now,

> you needn't do that now, daddy, it's alright,
> they don't make a sound anymore, you needn't
> do that, daddy, 'cos they don't make a sound
> anymore

44

27 October 1974

Charlie is three

NATASHA   Charlie hugs people because he doesn't like
them. That's why he hugs them

45

9 November 1974

NATASHA   you can't tie your two shoe laces at once
because you can't do two times at once

.   .   .

NATASHA   how long does forty minutes take?

46

November 1974

ADAM   there's going to be three of us
DADDY   yes
ADAM   mummy's going to have a baby
(*pause*)
aren't you proud of her?
DADDY   yes
ADAM   yes

47

25 November 1974

Evening

NATASHA	why are you looking down?
RONNIE	I'm feeling sad
NATASHA	why are you feeling sad?
RONNIE	I don't know
NATASHA	you don't know
RONNIE	I want to write things, but I don't seem able to
NATASHA	why are you not able to?
RONNIE	I don't know
NATASHA	what do you want to write?
RONNIE	I want to tell people what people tell me
NATASHA	maybe you can't remember what people tell you. Maybe you've forgotten what people tell you
RONNIE	well. You hear a *lot* of what people tell me. Can *you* remember what people tell me?*
NATASHA	yes. I can remember
RONNIE	people say so many things
NATASHA	yes I know
RONNIE	and what do they say?
NATASHA	they want to go home
RONNIE	Oh. Really
NATASHA	yes. They want to go home
RONNIE	but they don't know how to go home
NATASHA	I know
RONNIE	how can they go home, if they don't know the way home?

*Natasha is only allowed into my room when I'm seeing people if I don't know she's there. She has a pair of Tibetan house-shoes she calls "sneakers," which make no sound and usually make her invisible. She puts them on to sneak into my room and curl up under my desk.

NATASHA	I don't know
RONNIE	how can I tell them?
NATASHA	I don't know
RONNIE	that's why I'm so sad
NATASHA	Daddy?
RONNIE	Natasha?
NATASHA	are you going to write that down?
RONNIE	yes
NATASHA	I knew you would
RONNIE	it's difficult isn't it?
NATASHA	if they spent the night here, they would find their house
RONNIE	(*silence*)
NATASHA	you're not going to write that down are you?
RONNIE	probably not
NATASHA	I thought you wouldn't (*disapprovingly*)

48

Sitting on my lap

NATASHA	you can't remember one thing
RONNIE	Oh. what?
NATASHA	there's lots of things you can remember but there's one thing you can't remember
RONNIE	O there's lots and lots of things I can't remember
NATASHA	I know. But there's one thing you can't remember
RONNIE	what is the one thing I can't remember?
NATASHA	you were in here talking to one of the people who come to see you
RONNIE	what was it?
NATASHA	(*laughing*) I don't know
RONNIE	if you don't know what is the one thing I can't remember how do you know I can't remember it?
NATASHA	what did you say?
RONNIE	if you don't know what is the one thing I can't remember how do you know I can't remember it?
NATASHA	I don't know
RONNIE	you don't know how you know there's one thing I can't remember?
NATASHA	no
RONNIE	then how can you say that then?
NATASHA	there's one thing I do know
RONNIE	Oh. what's that?
NATASHA	first lady forward, second lady back first lady's finger up the second lady's crack
RONNIE	Oh really? and is there nothing else you know?

NATASHA	(*slowly*)
	Septimus Branigan he was there
	He put up a magnificent show
	He shoved his tagger up his arse
	And tied it in a bow
RONNIE	O is there nothing else you know than that?
NATASHA	I'm going to tell Adam something
	I'll be back

She runs off and comes back shortly

	I forgot one
RONNIE	don't tell me
NATASHA	landing on her tits
RONNIE	I don't want to talk about it
NATASHA	do you remember it?
RONNIE	yes
NATASHA	do you still remember it?
RONNIE	yes
NATASHA	say it then
RONNIE	I really don't want to. I'm sorry I told
	you these ones
NATASHA	come on Daddy
RONNIE	the minister's wife she was there
	she had us all in fits
	jumping off the mantelpiece
NATASHA	and landing on her tits
	and landing on her tits
	and landing on her tits
	(*peals of laughter*)

She runs off and comes back in a few seconds

	I've made up a few
RONNIE	O really? what?
NATASHA	two tomatoes crossing the road
RONNIE	you never made that up you heard it
	from someone

40

NATASHA	no I didn't. I made that one up
RONNIE	I've heard it before
NATASHA	No you haven't
	I made that one up myself

And off she runs again

49

After midnight

Natasha comes into my room trailing her quilt. It's dark apart from
a desk lamp. She stands silently for a while

NATASHA	When are you going to bed daddy?
DADDY	(*testily*)
	I don't know. Why?
NATASHA	I'm not going to bed till you go to bed
DADDY	(*gruffly*)
	you can go to bed whenever you like as long as I don't know you're up. I just want to work I don't want to hear you or see you anymore tonight, alright?
NATASHA	alright you'll have to carry me out
DADDY	I'm sorry Natasha. I don't feel like it
NATASHA	that's the only way you'll get me out of the room
DADDY	No
NATASHA	and you'll have to carry me all the way to my bed and snuggle me in
DADDY	(*softening*)
	alright as long as this is the last time. This is definitely the last time tonight
DADDY	(*picking her up*)
	promise
NATASHA	(*being carried*)
	promise
DADDY	(*tuggling her in*)
	you promised before
NATASHA	I know. The last time was the very very last time

DADDY	and this is the very very very last time
NATASHA	(*snuggling in*) say your prayers
DADDY	(*kissing her*) I mean it this time. Goodnight Natasha
NATASHA	(*as Daddy is walking away—calling out*) say your prayers
DADDY	(*at the door—in a loud whisper*) yes I will. And you say your prayers
NATASHA	goodnight Daddy
DADDY	goodnight Natasha

50

Natasha opens the door of my room and ushers in Charlie.
He slumps against the wall whimpering

ME	what's the matter Charlie?
CHARLIE	(*eventually*)
	I'm afraid of the Chinese puzzle
ME	Why?
CHARLIE	(*eventually*)
	there are baddies in it
ME	how do you mean?
CHARLIE	there are baddies in it
NATASHA	I gave it to the cat
ME	What! The Chinese puzzle!
NATASHA	Yes. I gave it to the cat. It's alright
	Charlie

Charlie runs off, looking more scared than ever

ME	what did he mean?
NATASHA	how?
ME	when he said there were baddies in it
NATASHA	it's a *Chinese* puzzle
ME	well?
NATASHA	the Chinese are baddies
ME	he thought there were actual baddies actually inside the Chinese puzzle
NATASHA	no he didn't
ME	you told him
NATASHA	no I didn't
ME	and now he'll think there are actual Chinese baddies inside the cat!
NATASHA	no he will not
ME	anyhow why do you say the Chinese are baddies?

NATASHA	I heard it on television
ME	really
NATASHA	they are baddies because they kill people
ME	there are some baddies everywhere
NATASHA	the Chinese are some baddies
ME	there are some baddies everywhere
NATASHA	no there're not

51

17 December 1974

Dinner

A lady is yattering on and on

NATASHA	do you hear what you're saying?
LADY	No (*startled*) Thank God! (*giggle*)
NATASHA	(*severely*)
	if you wiggle your ear with every mind in
	you your chair might go up

52

December 1974

Car drive from London to Devon

Adam and Natasha will not stop squabbling, squawking, squawling
in the back seat

JUTTA	if you don't shut up, I'm going to leave the pair of you
NATASHA	well go ahead then
JUTTA	just don't be so cheeky
NATASHA	I'm going to run away
JUTTA	well run away then
NATASHA	how can I run away when I don't know where I am?

53

5 January 1975

NATASHA	I hope I'm dead when I die

54

16 February 1975

NATASHA   what am I?
DADDY   you're half German
MUMMY   and half Scottish
NATASHA   half German?
MUMMY   and the other half of you is Scottish
NATASHA   what is the whole of me?
MUMMY   you're a funny mixture (*laughing*)
NATASHA   (*hitting Jutta with a piece of paper*)
             I'm not friends with you
JUTTA   O Natasha
NATASHA   it's not funny at all
JUTTA   I'm not laughing *at* you
NATASHA   yes you were
JUTTA   not in *that* way
NATASHA   I'm not friends with you
JUTTA   I'm not laughing *at* you
NATASHA   yes you were I don't like you anymore
RONNIE   there's one from mummy
             and one from daddy
             and the two of them become one
             and the whole of that one is you
JUTTA   it's absolutely terrifying
RONNIE   what is?
JUTTA   crushing all that into one

Natasha leaves the room and comes back in a little while with two
pieces of paper, out of the middle of each of which she has cut two
circles

NATASHA   here is one hole for you (*giving one
             piece to Jutta*) and here's one hole for
             you (*giving one piece to me*)

JUTTA RONNIE	} O thank you Natasha
NATASHA	(*to Jutta*) I give up the fight

And they are friends again

55

3 April 1975

Adam is standing looking seriously puzzled

DADDY	what is it?
ADAM	this stairway wasn't even *here* until they put it here

56

NATASHA   God bless mummy and daddy and
Adam and Natasha and
God bless everything. Goodbye

57

May 1975

Evening

NATASHA   what's that book
RONNIE   that's the Bible
NATASHA   what's the Bible?
RONNIE   it's a book of stories about God and us
NATASHA   does it tell stories about God?
RONNIE   yes
NATASHA   are these stories about God?
RONNIE   they are stories that some people say
               are about God
NATASHA   are they *really* about God?
RONNIE   I don't know
NATASHA   will you read me one?

I read her the first twenty-two verses of Genesis

NATASHA   is it all about God?
RONNIE   yes
NATASHA   has this page got God in it?
               (*leafing through the pages and picking out
               pages at random*)
RONNIE   yes
NATASHA   and this page?
RONNIE   yes
NATASHA   and this page?
RONNIE   yes
NATASHA   and this page?
RONNIE   yes
NATASHA   I think God is on every page
RONNIE   He's given different names but
               He can't really have a name
               we cannot really name Him

NATASHA	I know, He's not a girlie *(pause)* nor a boy *(pause)* you don't know whether He's a boy or a girl do you?
RONNIE	no
NATASHA	no one knows God but He knows **us,** and He knows Himself
RONNIE	how do you know that?
NATASHA	I don't know how I know it
RONNIE	but you know it
NATASHA	Yes. And no one can see God but He can see us and He can see Himself He could be in this house He could be outside the door He could knock on the door but He would have to knock very hard for us to hear Him, wouldn't he?
RONNIE	yes
NATASHA	No we don't hear the God-knocks *(with a sad chuckle)* He would have to knock on the *God*-door!
RONNIE	and where shall we say the God-door is?
NATASHA	how would someone like me know where the God-door is?
RONNIE	do you think God minds us talking about Him like this?
NATASHA	No. He doesn't mind *(pause)* maybe we can see *through* Him, like your glasses *(laughing, seriously, quizzically)* *(pause)* do you think so?
RONNIE	I don't know *(pause)* see *through* Him but not see Him *(musing)*
NATASHA	He can see Himself. We can't see Him. Some *gods* can see Him. He can see us.

(she is leafing through the Bible as she is saying this)
I can't look at every page tonight
otherwise I'll get to stay up late and
be tired so I'll go now daddy

RONNIE   alright Natasha

We are in a large delightful bedroom. Natasha had earlier brought up a spray of flowers: "These are for you and Jutta." Now, after the foregoing conversation, she sits on the bed, in silence, contemplating me on the floor, surrounded with sheaves of paper, reading what I have written, scoring out, tearing up, cutting and piecing together, arranging and rearranging.

NATASHA	you've done an awful lot of writing
RONNIE	I know
NATASHA	I think you've almost finished your book*
RONNIE	I'm very glad to hear it. I sure hope so Are you sure?
NATASHA	yes. you've almost finished it (*kisses*) I'm going downstairs now
RONNIE	alright. thanks for the flowers goodnight
NATASHA	I'm not going to bed, but you can say goodnight if you want to
RONNIE	goodnight Natasha
NATASHA	goodnight Ronnie

* She was right. I was almost at end of what turned out to be *The Facts of Life*.

52

58

25 May 1975

NATASHA   can I jump on you?
DAVID   yes
NATASHA   are you sure?
DAVID   yes
NATASHA   I'm five now you know not four
           and three quarters

59

15 July 1975

NATASHA Tony says his father is a giant.
he is bigger than Joan [her teacher]
ME is he bigger than me?
NATASHA I don't know

       ·   ·   ·

She has been measuring people's heights by a length of string and a tape rule. She wants me to tell her how many of my hands length she is. She is seven of my hands long.

60

July 1975

Natasha explains to Adam

> Harry can't marry his mummy and
> Lucy can't marry her daddy
> and you can't marry me

61

Natasha persuaded Jutta recently to buy her a small screwdriver. It is nicely proportioned with a blue handle

NATASHA	do you like my screwdriver?
RONNIE	yes I do. It's very sweet
NATASHA	do you think it's *very* sweet?
RONNIE	yes. It's very pretty
NATASHA	it's the *smallest* screwdriver in the house. Isn't it? Is it the smallest screwdriver in the house?
RONNIE	it might well be. I'm not absolutely sure
NATASHA	if you need to screw anything, you can use it. I'll let you use it whenever you want to
RONNIE	thank you very much
NATASHA	will you keep it for me?
RONNIE	alright. we can put it on my desk, and you can take it whenever you like
NATASHA	alright

She left it on my desk for a few days, sometimes taking it away and putting it back. Then she kept it herself. Last night she went to bed with it

NATASHA	(*as Jutta is tuggling her in*) I'm going to sleep with my little screwdriver. Thank you for giving my little screwdriver. I like it. It's the smallest one in the whole house

62

Early evening

Jutta and I are sitting around talking with friends.
Natasha comes into the room with boxing gloves on, and a pair for
me

NATASHA   will you have a boxing match?
RONNIE   no not just now. I'm talking just now.
           I don't feel like it just now
NATASHA   will you have a boxing match later?
RONNIE   well, maybe
NATASHA   you have a boxing match with me later,
           when you don't need to talk, alright
           Daddy? You have a boxing match with me
           when you don't *need* to talk anymore,
           alright Daddy?
RONNIE   alright Natasha

                  .   .   .

NATASHA   I might marry Matthew (*reflective pause*)
           And if he won't marry me, I might
           marry Anthony (*another reflective pause*)
           And if he won't marry me, I might
           marry Andrew (*long pause*)
RONNIE   and if he wouldn't marry you, whom
           would you marry?
NATASHA   if he wouldn't marry me, I might marry—
           Michael
RONNIE   and if he wouldn't marry you?
JUTTA   you haven't mentioned Charlie
NATASHA   Mmmmmmm. I'll marry who I like

63

Natasha wants me to make her a bow with a stick of wood and a length of string.
While I'm fixing it

NATASHA	am I allowed a piece of wood that's longer than my arm?
RONNIE	why not? this is about the length of your arm, isn't it?
NATASHA	but am I?
RONNIE	what?
NATASHA	*allowed* it if it's *longer* than my arm?
RONNIE	I suppose so. There's no rule against it, as far as I know. So yes. You're allowed it

She still looks unconvinced

64

Jutta is cradling Max

NATASHA   *(softly and sweetly to herself,*
           but loud enough for Jutta to hear her)
           I have a lovely mummy I have a kind
           mummy I have a beautiful mummy called
           Jutta
           (and then with no pause, suddenly,
           in a sharp peremptory tone)
           Have you put new sheets in my bed?

JUTTA   not yet. I will. Later.

NATASHA   are you putting Max in *my* bed?

JUTTA   yes

NATASHA   *(reproachfully)*
           you usually put him in *Adam's* bed

JUTTA   *(on the defensive)*
           not always

NATASHA   and you said I could hold him as well as
           Adam and now you let Adam hold him and not
           me and it's not fair

Jutta without a word hands Max to Natasha

NATASHA   *(rocking Max)*
           you're beautiful
           I think you're beautiful
           I think you're a queen
                   everyone wouldn't
           I think you're beautiful
           I think you're a queen
                   everyone wouldn't

RONNIE   you think he's a what?

NATASHA   I don't want to tell you

RONNIE	a queen?
NATASHA	yes

I shouldn't have said anything. She started to sing him "My Grandfather's Clock."

65

JUTTA   (*to Adam and Natasha in a quiet commanding voice which brooks no nonsense*)
Tidy your beds, straighten your pillows, fold your sheets

They set about it

ADAM	you're just doing this because you have to
NATASHA	No. I'm doing it because I want to
ADAM	you're doing it because you have to
NATASHA	No. I'm doing it because I want to
ADAM	mummy told us to so we have to
NATASHA	I still don't have to if I don't want to
ADAM	Oh yes you do
NATASHA	no I don't
ADAM	you have to
NATASHA	I don't have to I want to

66

Adam has just come into the room with two model aircraft he has made. After Jutta and I have admired them

ADAM	I like this one better
RONNIE	why?
ADAM	because *this* one (*the other one*) is only a civilian plane
RONNIE	what's wrong with that?
ADAM	it doesn't carry any rockets
RONNIE	it's a very nice design
ADAM	O I like the design of it. But it's only got these bombs (*pointing to two under each wing*) and they are only to be used if *absolutely* necessary
JUTTA	rockets and bombs aren't particularly beautiful
ADAM	well I like this one better because it's a *war* plane

67

16 August 1975

Jutta gave Natasha a present of a large (neither inflatable nor deflatable), many-colored ball a few days ago

For the last three days, first thing on waking, she has come into our (Jutta's, my, and Max's) bedroom with the ball, complaining that it is getting smaller

NATASHA	the ball is smaller
JUTTA	no it's not Natasha. It's exactly the same size
NATASHA	no. The ball is getting smaller
RONNIE	you're getting bigger every day, so the ball may seem to you to be getting smaller
JUTTA	she is growing at such a rate these days
NATASHA	the ball is getting smaller

68

August 1975

NATASHA   why did the boy throw the clock out
the window?

ADAM   because he wanted to see time fly

. . .

A patient of mine once ate her favorite record.
I asked Jutta

Why did that girl eat the record?

JUTTA   because she wanted the music inside her

69

It's a sultry summer day by a waterfall.
Natasha is sitting naked on a rock, singing to herself

> I'm going away
> I'm sad to say
> for many a day
> (*pause*)
>
> I'm going away
> for many a day
> unless you call
> (*longer pause, but not very long*)
>
> Please don't call
> for I want to stay
> away
> for many a day

70

DEVON   *August 1975*

A hot summer morning

I am absorbed in reading and brooding over the *Agamemnon* of
Aeschylus, deep in the labyrinth of that dark legend

Someone is tugging my beard

       Daddy?

Natasha must have been standing there for some time

       Daddy? (*twirling my beard*) Have you
       forgotten how to smile, daddy?
       Ah! That's a smile. Cheerio daddy

71

26 August 1975

NATASHA	can you pick up David?
RONNIE	yes
NATASHA	and can David pick up you?
RONNIE	yes
NATASHA	you can pick up David and David can pick up you?
RONNIE	yes
NATASHA	and what about Arthur?
RONNIE	David can pick up Arthur and Arthur can pick up David
NATASHA	and what about you?
RONNIE	Arthur can pick up me and I can pick up Arthur
NATASHA	Oh

72

27 August 1975

NATASHA   (*contemplating Max*)
                 now I'm not the littlest one anymore

73

                                                August 1975

Natasha has become intrigued by a cubical box.
She has been turning it around looking at it curiously, from all
angles.

Now she has cut out two of its sides, and has been showing it to
everyone around. She is fairly jumping with excitement

          Look daddy. If you look *through* it,
          you can't see the bottom of it

74

August 1975

NATASHA   I've found a wiggly tooth

DADDY   let me feel it. O yes

NATASHA   yes that's the naughty tooth. I'm
not going to tell anyone about it

DADDY   why not?

NATASHA   I've told everyone here about it. But
I'm not going to tell anyone in London
about it

DADDY   No?

NATASHA   No. Because it's a secret and if I told
everyone about it, it wouldn't be a
secret anymore, would it?

DADDY   no I suppose it wouldn't

75

MONDAY   *1 September 1975*

At breakfast

ADAM	when I'm ten you'll be eight and when
	I'm thirteen you'll be eleven because
	I'm two years older than you
NATASHA	I can't get older than you but
	I can get bigger than you
ADAM	you can get bigger than me but I
	doubt it
NATASHA	you doubt it
ADAM	Yes. I doubt it

Later that morning

JUTTA	would you go over to the house and
	bring back a bottle of milk and some butter
	please Adam

Adam continues doing what he is doing

JUTTA	Adam! how many times do I have to ask you
	to do something
ADAM	what?
JUTTA	would you go over to the house and bring
	back a bottle of milk and some butter
	please
ADAM	No
JUTTA	Ronnie!
RONNIE	what?
JUTTA	I've asked Adam twice to do something
	and he just won't do it
RONNIE	to do what?

JUTTA	to go and get milk and butter from the house
RONNIE	didn't you hear mummy ask you?
ADAM	yes but I don't have to
RONNIE	she was *asking* you nicely, I'm *telling* you
ADAM	you mean I can't refuse
DADDY	you can refuse, but if you do I'll be very unpleasant to you
ADAM	in what way?
DADDY	in *some* way
ADAM	in *what* way?
DADDY	just do it
ADAM	but in *what* way?
DADDY	you won't get any biscuits today

He started calculating. My eyes narrowed. My tone changed

	just get moving or you're in big trouble with me right now
ADAM	you mean I've got to
DADDY	yes

He went

76

In a compartment on the train

NATASHA	I've cleaned my hands, can I touch Max?
RONNIE	no
NATASHA	ho ho ho. Yes
RONNIE	no
NATASHA	Ronnie said no is yes yes is no ho ho ho no means yes and yes means no Ronnie said yes
RONNIE	*No* Natasha
NATASHA	alright daddy

77

Playing ball with Natasha

DADDY   three more throws
NATASHA   six more

after three more

NATASHA   three more
DADDY   well alright

after these three more

NATASHA   one more
DADDY   well this is the last one

after the last one

NATASHA   one more
DADDY   well this is the very last one

after the very last one

NATASHA   one more
DADDY   well this the very very last one

after the very very last one

NATASHA   I'm running off now

And away she ran, with never a glance behind her
No very very very last one

78

September 1975

Evening

Suddenly I was tired. I had to stretch out. Just as I lay down

NATASHA   will you untie my balloon?
DADDY   sorry Natasha I'm tired
NATASHA   but I want you to untie my balloon
DADDY   later, in about ten minutes maybe
           but not now
NATASHA   Ooh daddy but I want you to do it now
DADDY   sorry not now not now. I've got to shut
           my eyes and not move *anything* for a few
           minutes
           (*silence for several seconds*)
NATASHA   do you think one balloon is enough?
DADDY   it depends what for
NATASHA   when it's my birthday would you buy
           me one balloon?

Adam's birthday was yesterday. There had been dozens of balloons
at his birthday party

DADDY   O I would get you a *packet* of balloons
           As many as Adam. More if you want
NATASHA   and how many would you get me if it
           wasn't my birthday?
DADDY   I would get you a packet of balloons
           if you really wanted anytime
NATASHA   but do you think one's enough?

I was puzzled. I said nothing

NATASHA   I think one's enough

Then she burst the one she was holding. Accidentally.
I startled

> O sorry daddy
> O I popped my balloon! sorry
> daddy (*and she ran off to mummy*)
> mummy I popped my balloon, mummy I
> popped my balloon

79

SATURDAY   *13 September 1975*

NATASHA   can everyone in the whole world
               smile?

80

ADAM	I might just make one of my inventions
RONNIE	what inventions?
ADAM	I have made many inventions
RONNIE	how many?
ADAM	many
NATASHA	four
RONNIE	and what are they?
ADAM	my first invention was a space capsule with many capabilities
RONNIE	o yes
ADAM	and my second invention was a darikrex
RONNIE	a what?
ADAM	a darikrex*
RONNIE	I have never heard of a darikrex
ADAM	I invented the name
RONNIE	and what is it
ADAM	it's a machine that shoots out of three tubes
RONNIE	shoots what out?
ADAM	bananas, peas, and tomatoes
RONNIE	really!?
ADAM	and my third invention was a carriage for crushing snow. It will have a specially designed cabin
JUTTA	will it be cold?
ADAM	it will be centrally heated, to avoid having to use electricity.

---

* I made this entry on September 18. I'm not sure I got his invention phonetically correct. The following day (September 19) there was a report in the *International Herald Tribune* on work by Drs. Herbert and Irving Dardik on umbilical cord transplant surgery.

81

Morning

NATASHA	daddy
DADDY	yes Natasha
NATASHA	I still don't know how to do knots
	in shoes
DADDY	you soon will
NATASHA	I know. But Daddy.
	I put my shoe on *before* Adam

Evening

NATASHA	(*swishing her arm*)
	does a car go faster than that
DADDY	yes. I think so. I'm not sure, actually
NATASHA	how fast does my arm go?
DADDY	I'm not sure

82

4 November 1975

As we were sitting around the table with friends after dinner, Natasha came in with a bottle

NATASHA	look
RONNIE	oh
NATASHA	do you like my bottle?
RONNIE	it's alright
NATASHA	I'm collecting bottles
RONNIE	oh why?
NATASHA	so I'll have *more* than Adam
RONNIE	how interesting. And what else is "more than Adam"?
NATASHA	after I've had a bath, I pour *more* water over my hair
RONNIE	really I didn't know that
NATASHA	and I'm going to fill all my bottles up with water
RONNIE	then you'll *have more* water than Adam
NATASHA	yes (*clinching it*)

83

12 November 1975

Late afternoon

As I was walking home I met Natasha and Matthew. Natasha said "Hello Daddy." We kissed. I walked on hearing her say to Matthew "That's my daddy."

About thirty minutes later, Natasha came in the bathroom while I was having a bath. She stood looking at me. And continued to stand looking

DADDY	Well?
NATASHA	are you the same daddy I kissed in the street?
RONNIE	(*irritably*) yes (*pause*) YES! Why?
NATASHA	are you the same daddy?
RONNIE	YES! why? Do you think I may not be?
NATASHA	your hair is shorter
RONNIE	yes it's shorter
NATASHA	it's *grown* shorter (*doubtfully*)
RONNIE	no it hasn't grown shorter (*pause*) I had it *cut* shorter (*she doesn't believe me. I feel a pang of panic*) yes! It's true. There was a man in here (*the first time this has ever happened*) who cuts hair. He just cut my hair before you came home
NATASHA	O *I* see. It *looks* shorter because you have *shampoo* on.

(That's a relief. At least she's discarded the theory that I'm a different daddy.)

RONNIE	yes. But it is *actually* shorter because it was *cut* shorter
NATASHA	No. I see. It *looks* shorter and you—*look* different

And she went out of the bathroom

84

WEDNESDAY *12 November 1975*

ADAM	what did one candle say to the other candle?
DADDY	I don't know
ADAM	I'm going out tonight

85

Evening

JUTTA	(*teasing*)
	I'm going away
ADAM	(*laughing*)
	you can't do that because I love you
	and if you go away I'll kill you

Same evening. Later

NATASHA	I wish I could marry you daddy
DADDY	Oh Natasha, we can't
NATASHA	I know because you're married to mummy
DADDY	even if I weren't, we couldn't
	because you're my daughter and I'm
	your daddy and daughters and daddys
	aren't allowed to get married
NATASHA	we're in the same family
DADDY	yes
NATASHA	but mummy's in the same family, so how
	can you be married to her?
DADDY	when mummy and I met she wasn't your
	mummy and we were not members of the
	same family and she isn't my daughter
	so it was alright to get married and have
	children
ADAM	by putting your penis into mummy's
	vagina
DADDY	and become a family and get married
JUTTA	it's bedtime now
DADDY	yes it's past your bedtime
NATASHA	but I'm not sleepy

DADDY   I never said you were. Anyway. Kisses. (*kisses*)
             and you're to go through to your room and be
             quiet
ADAM   (*kissing Jutta*)
             Natasha would like to marry daddy,
             and I would like to marry you.

86

20 November 1975

I am sitting reading Lovejoy's *The Great Chain of Being*.
Natasha is holding Max, whirling around.
Jutta announces "Dinner!"

Natasha yells "charge!" and sets off at a gallop, but stops after three
or four steps

>Sorry Max. I didn't know I had you in my
>arms. Charge!

And resumes her gallop, this time holding Max, as she says these
days, "knowingly" or "rememberingly."

87

At dinner

NATASHA   (*to Jutta and me*)
           were you two born together?
RONNIE   did we come out of the same mummy
           at the same time?
NATASHA   yes
RONNIE   no we were born at different times,
           different places, and came out of two
           different mummies who are your two
           grannies

TV war film

ADAM   change it
JUTTA   keep it on I want to see it
ADAM   you killer-lover!

88

ADAM   what is black and white and red all over
NATASHA   I don't know
ADAM   a newspaper
NATASHA   it's not red all over
ADAM   of course it's read all over

But Natasha didn't "get it," quite

89

2 December 1975

ADAM   let's do a handstand
NATASHA   O yes that's what I was thinking of
                 twenty-five years ago

90

NATASHA are you older than Margaret?
JUTTA   yes Margaret is two weeks younger
         than me I think
NATASHA how old are you?
JUTTA   I'm thirty-six
NATASHA are you older than Adam?
JUTTA   of course I am, Natasha
NATASHA I'm not the youngest in this house
         now. Even if Max gets older he'll never
         get older than me. I'll always be older
         than him won't I mummy?
JUTTA   yes Natasha
NATASHA is daddy older than Arthur?
JUTTA   yes Natasha

91

Xmas

ADAM   (*exulting after two glasses of wine*)
            Come to Heaven!
NATASHA   don't be silly, Heaven is dead!

92

I'm in the bath. Natasha is standing beside it

NATASHA	(*pointing to my right knee*) what's that?
RONNIE	that's a birthmark
NATASHA	what's it for?
RONNIE	it's just there. My dad had one on *his* right knee
NATASHA	what did you want it for?
RONNIE	I didn't want it. I just got it

She says nothing. She is not persuaded

	you've got brown eyes. You've got them
NATASHA	but I *wanted* brown eyes
RONNIE	and that's why you got them?
NATASHA	yes
RONNIE	Oh

I ponder over this information for a little

	Well, is there anything about you you didn't want?
NATASHA	no
RONNIE	you wanted to be a girlie and not a boyie?
NATASHA	(*indignantly*) yes
RONNIE	nothing at *all* you didn't want?

Natasha's eyes roll right up so I see only their whites, as she scans all the possibilities. After a long pause

NATASHA	I didn't want to be itchy

93

As I'm setting off for a Chinese restaurant to bring a meal back for the family

NATASHA	will you give me a carry on your shoulders?
RONNIE	O yes. But it's a cold winter's night outside
NATASHA	I know. Will there be ghosts?
RONNIE	there may be
NATASHA	there may be ghosts out there?
RONNIE	have you ever met a ghost?
NATASHA	no
RONNIE	how do you know?
NATASHA	I know
RONNIE	but if you've never met a ghost, how do you know what a ghost is like?
NATASHA	I know
RONNIE	what's a ghost like?
NATASHA	it's white. And it scares people. The white comes up from under it
RONNIE	oh
NATASHA	if it comes down *to* its feet it's not a ghost
RONNIE	how do you know that?
NATASHA	I've seen it on television
RONNIE	O come on! Most of what's on the television is just what people make up— it's not necessarily *true*
NATASHA	o but I know that if it has white over it down to its ankles it isn't a real ghost
RONNIE	that's correct. You don't know how you know that, or do you?
NATASHA	no I don't
RONNIE	but you know it?
NATASHA	yes

RONNIE	you know quite a lot of things
	I don't know
NATASHA	I know
RONNIE	and there's quite a lot you know
	and don't know that you know it
NATASHA	I know
RONNIE	I don't think I know more than you
	know

Later, coming out of the restaurant

NATASHA	the sky is red
RONNIE	I wish there weren't these streetlights,
	then we could really see the sky
NATASHA	I wish the sky was down here
RONNIE	and then? then we could fly on it
NATASHA	I would lie on it

94

14 February 1976

Natasha and Adam have been quarrelling

NATASHA   I wish he were dead
JUTTA   Oh Natasha
NATASHA   I wish his seed had been crushed and he
           never had been
JUTTA   but Natasha! Adam's your brother
           and you would miss him
NATASHA   I *want* to miss him

95

14 March 1976

This morning Natasha was angry at Jutta and me because we shouted at her for shouting

NATASHA	(*to Jutta*)
	why do you have to lie like that?
JUTTA	I don't lie
NATASHA	you tell a lie every day
JUTTA	no I don't
NATASHA	you tell millions of lies
RONNIE	what lies?
NATASHA	I'm not telling you anything

. . .

I had promised Adam and Natasha I would give them some sweets, if

NATASHA	daddy when are we going to get some sweets?
DADDY	when mummy comes back
NATASHA	is she bringing them back?
DADDY	no. When mummy comes back, I'll give you and Adam some money to go out and get some sweets
NATASHA	you cheat!
DADDY	why?
NATASHA	you said you would *give* us the sweets
DADDY	ok when mummy comes back I'll go out and get some sweets, and bring them back and give them to you and Adam—is that alright?

NATASHA	yes
DADDY	if you take care of Max till mummy comes back ok?
NATASHA	yes

We each kept our side of the bargain

96

Last night

NATASHA	are you staying upstairs?
DADDY	no I think I'll go downstairs in about two minutes
NATASHA	I thought you were going to say that
DADDY	you could stay up here
NATASHA	no I'll stay with you. Where you go I'll go if you go downstairs I'll go downstairs if you go upstairs I'll go upstairs
DADDY	you could stay upstairs when I go downstairs
NATASHA	then I'll get a creepy feeling
DADDY	what sort of creepy feeling?
NATASHA	a creepy feeling like there was a ghost upstairs
DADDY	what sort of a ghost?
NATASHA	a *real* ghost

97

NATASHA	why did the ink run?
DADDY	I don't know
NATASHA	because it was a repelling pencil
DADDY	a what?
NATASHA	a *repelling* pencil
DADDY	I've never heard of a *repelling* pencil
NATASHA	I know you haven't

Later

NATASHA	have you written that one down?
DADDY	no
NATASHA	are you going to?
DADDY	well I'm not quite sure about it
NATASHA	it was a *repelling* pencil
DADDY	but it doesn't sound quite the same as the others
ADAM	like what's the quickest way to double your money?
DADDY	fold it
ADAM	why do birds fly south?
NATASHA	because it's too far to walk
ADAM	what is a sleeping bull?
NATASHA	a bulldozer. It was a repelling pencil!

98

Evening

NATASHA	when are we going home?
DADDY	the day after tomorrow
NATASHA	when is that?
DADDY	it's tonight and
NATASHA	two sleeps
DADDY	it's tonight and one sleep
NATASHA	it's two sleeps in all
DADDY	you sleep tonight that's one sleep and then it's tomorrow. At the end of tomorrow you have another sleep and when you wake up from *that* sleep it's the day *after* tomorrow and that's the day we go home
NATASHA	I have a sleep tonight for tomorrow and another sleep for the day we go home. That's two sleeps
DADDY	right do you know what's the name of tomorrow?
NATASHA	no
DADDY	do you want me to tell you?
NATASHA	yes
DADDY	the name of tomorrow is Saturday
NATASHA	O Saturday
DADDY	Yes. And do you know the name of the day after tomorrow?
NATASHA	No. What is it?
DADDY	Sunday
NATASHA	Sunday
DADDY	and do you know the name of the day that comes after Sunday?

NATASHA	Saturday
DADDY	No. Saturday comes *before* Sunday. The name of the day that comes *after* Sunday is Monday
NATASHA	Monday
DADDY	and the day after that?
NATASHA	Tuesday
DADDY	and after that?
NATASHA	Wednesday
DADDY	and after that?
NATASHA	(*thinks*)
DADDY	Thursday, and after that?
NATASHA	Friday
DADDY	and after that?
NATASHA	Saturday
DADDY	and what day is this?
NATASHA	Monday
DADDY	no it comes before Saturday because Saturday's tomorrow
NATASHA	Friday. It's Friday

Later

NATASHA	it's going to be my birthday soon
JUTTA	that's right, only fourteen days
RONNIE	what date?
JUTTA	the 24th April
NATASHA	I can't wait till it's my birthday
RONNIE	what's the hurry
NATASHA	I can't wait to get all my presents I'm going to get more presents than Adam, aren't I?
RONNIE	not necessarily. Adam gets presents on his birthday and you get presents on yours. I don't know who will get most
NATASHA	but I'll get more presents than Adam on my birthday

RONNIE	O yes you don't have to worry about that. When it's Adam's birthday he gets all the presents and you don't get any and on your birthday you'll get all the presents and Adam won't get any
NATASHA	but Omilie [Jutta's mother] may send him a present
JUTTA	that's right. She normally sends something to everyone
RONNIE	well you'll still get *more* than Adam on your birthday

Natasha wants a *toy* walkie-talkie and a *real* calculating machine for her birthday

99

10 April 1976

NATASHA	you're older than Jutta and you're bigger than Jutta
ME	uh huh
NATASHA	Jutta can never get older than you (*reassuringly*) but she could get bigger than you
ME	no she cannot get bigger than me
NATASHA	she might. (*pause*) why not?
ME	because we've both stopt growing
NATASHA	you've both stopt growing?
ME	yes
NATASHA	I haven't stopt growing. I've got a *lot* of growing to do yet
ME	I know
	(*pause*)
NATASHA	Daddy? How old are you?
ME	forty-eight
	(*pause*)
NATASHA	when will I stop growing?
ME	I don't know maybe some time around eighteen
NATASHA	is that how old Jutta is?
ME	no. Jutta's twice as old as eighteen. She's thirty-six
NATASHA	eighteen and forty-eight sound the same word
ME	they don't sound *quite* the same word when you're forty-eight
	(*pause*)
NATASHA	there's a man who said Adam and I are younger than we are
ME	O really. How could you be younger than you are?

NATASHA	I don't know that's just what he said
ME	did you ask him what he meant?
NATASHA	no I did not
ME	what was he like?
NATASHA	his fingers cracked when he moved them fast like this *(suddenly a most convincingly alarming demonstration)* and not when he moved them slowly
ME	and what do you think he meant?
NATASHA	I expect he meant what he said
ME	you wouldn't care to put what he meant into any other words?
NATASHA	No. I do not care to put it into any other words

NATASHA	when's your birthday?
DADDY	in October
NATASHA	how long is that?
DADDY	about half a year
NATASHA	when is mine?
DADDY	yours is almost a year away
NATASHA	is yours before mine then?
DADDY	yes
NATASHA	will it always be before mine?
DADDY	no, after I have my birthday, your birthday will be before mine

Breakfast

DADDY	Natasha. You don't need all that muessli
NATASHA	yes I do
DADDY	you're only taking all that amount because Adam took that amount
NATASHA	I'm taking *more* than Adam
DADDY	but you're not going to eat all that are you? you should take only what you're going to eat
NATASHA	I'm going to *eat more* than Adam
DADDY	but it's just what *you* want to eat it isn't a question of how much *Adam* eats
NATASHA	yes it is

101

At dinner

DADDY	Adam. I heard you say to Natasha
ADAM	O I know I know
DADDY	you said to Natasha
ADAM	when?
DADDY	at breakfast, on Saturday morning
ADAM	O I know I know I was just joking
DADDY	you said
ADAM	I didn't
DADDY	you said to Natasha that if she swore to God and broke her word God would hate her
ADAM	no I didn't. I said if she made a promise to God and didn't keep it, it's a sin
DADDY	I heard you say
ADAM	that was just joking. I never said anything like that
JUTTA	he's a real wriggler. He'll try to wriggle his way out of anything
ADAM	I was just joking
DADDY	just joking about that sort of thing is a sin
ADAM	I never said anything like that
DADDY	well don't ever again

102

NATASHA   daddy would you undo my button,
because when I undo it, it ends up
being done up

103

Last night

ADAM	Can I have £3 for the school?
DADDY	what for?
ADAM	I'm making a radio set with Frank, and we need some parts
DADDY	Oh
ADAM	yes. Frank's paid for them out of his money
DADDY	O well I suppose so—who's Frank anyway?
ADAM	Frank knows all sort of things—about science, birds; he knows the names of all the birds, and stars and astronomy. You would really like to talk to Frank; and he knows about trees and . . .
DADDY	uh huh but *what* is Frank then?
ADAM	Frank's the headmaster of the secondary school
DADDY	O really! Frank. He's the headmaster. Frank. what's he like?
ADAM	he sometimes gets angry
DADDY	O does he? what happens then?
ADAM	he starts to shout. He shouts
DADDY	what?
ADAM	he shouts "stop it!"
DADDY	stop what?
ADAM	O he doesn't like us carrying on making a lot of noise—messing things up— breaking things. You would like to talk to him about science, about the stars, and about the galaxies, and nebulae, and about trees, and birds.

THURSDAY *13 May 1976*

NATASHA	daddy?
DADDY	yes Natasha
NATASHA	do people tell the truth on television?
DADDY	sometimes they do and sometimes they don't
NATASHA	when do they tell the truth?
DADDY	there is no way of knowing that for sure
NATASHA	do they tell the truth when its *The News?*
DADDY	sometimes they do and sometimes they don't
NATASHA	sometimes they tell lies and sometimes they just tell the truth?
DADDY	yep

105

15 May 1976

NATASHA	daddy?
DADDY	uh huh?
NATASHA	when's your birthday?
DADDY	my birthday's in October
NATASHA	is it tomorrow?
DADDY	O no. October is a lot of tomorrows away (*pause*) why do you think it's tomorrow?
NATASHA	because you've been waiting so long
DADDY	but you wait just as long
NATASHA	no I don't
DADDY	everyone waits the same number of sleeps, or days between birthdays (*pause*) Do you think some people wait longer than others?
NATASHA	yes

May 1976

Max is crying. Jutta is out. I want to work

DADDY   Natasha! Will you take Max for half an
                  hour

There is no reply

DADDY   Natasha!

No reply

DADDY   Natasha, if you take Max for half an
                  hour I'll give you 5p
NATASHA   alright

She takes Max. After ten minutes

NATASHA   how many minutes now?
DADDY   ten minutes
NATASHA   but ten minutes is more than half an
                  hour
DADDY   no it isn't

She swings Max up and down, up and down, and with every down
swing

NATASHA   all the way down to God
DADDY   what did you say?
NATASHA   nothing
DADDY   all the way *down* to God?
NATASHA   yes (*laughing*)
DADDY   how do you mean?
NATASHA   I was talking to Max
DADDY   well say it again so I know what
                  you mean
NATASHA   I don't want to say it again
                  'cos I've forgotten it already

107

16 May 1976

N<small>ATASHA</small>	mummy, does God know everything?
M<small>UMMY</small>	I don't know
N<small>ATASHA</small>	do fairies go up to God?
M<small>UMMY</small>	I don't know
N<small>ATASHA</small>	Adam says they do (*pause*)

but they can come down again and see
their mummies, and they can go to
church, and sing to God:
and then they go to their homes
underground

108

7 June 1976

Adam is ringing our new front door bell, which chimes, for fun.

I hear myself shouting

       Stop that. Don't do that again unless I
       know it isn't you

NATASHA	if everyone always has their birthday on the same date, how does anyone get older than anyone else?
DADDY	no one ever gets older than anyone else
NATASHA	Oh!
DADDY	and no one ever gets younger than anyone else
NATASHA	Oh!
	(*pause*)
DADDY	No one gets older than anyone else *because* everyone always has their birthday on the same date
NATASHA	Oh

She still hasn't "got" it

Thursday   *20 May 1976*

Dinner

Pussycat jumps on the table and sniffs at the cheese

Daddy	pussycat!
Mummy	yes pussycat! take him off. He may have something
Natasha	what?
Mummy	some germs that are bad for us
Natasha	you've just made me unhungry
Daddy	how?
Natasha	the soup's changed its taste
Daddy	the soup's the same though it tastes different to you
Natasha	no it isn't, the soup's changed
Daddy	mummy's soup hasn't changed
Natasha	yes it has
Daddy	mine's the same
Natasha	well mine's different. I don't want it now
Daddy	the soup's the same. Mummy's remark about the cat made a difference to you but not to the soup
Natasha	well how does that make the *soup* taste different?

111

9 June 1976

(*Slowly*)

NATASHA	Monday Tuesday Wednesday Friday Saturday
JUTTA	No. Monday Tuesday Wednesday *Thursday* Friday Saturday *Sunday*
NATASHA	Monday Tuesday Wednesday Friday Saturday Sunday
JUTTA	No. Monday Tuesday Wednesday *Thursday* Friday Saturday Sunday
NATASHA	Monday Tuesday Wednesday Thursday Saturday Friday Sunday
JUTTA	No. Monday Tuesday Wednesday Thursday *Friday Saturday* Sunday
NATASHA	Sunday Monday Tuesday Wednesday Friday Saturday Sunday
JUTTA	No. Sunday Monday Tuesday Wednesday Thursday Friday *Saturday*
NATASHA	Sunday Tuesday Wednesday Friday Saturday Sunday
JUTTA	No! Sunday *Monday* Tuesday Wednesday *Thursday* Friday Saturday
RONNIE	Natasha
NATASHA	yes
RONNIE	Natasha

(*Presto e poco a poco accel. a prestissimo*)

	Monday Tuesday Wednesday Thursday Friday Saturday Sunday
NATASHA	Monday Tuesday Wednesday
RONNIE	Thursday Friday Saturday Sunday
NATASHA	Thursday Friday Saturday Sunday
RONNIE	Wednesday Thursday Friday
NATASHA	Wednesday Friday Thursday

RONNIE	Wednesday Thursday Friday
NATASHA	Wednesday Thursday Friday
RONNIE	Wednesday Thursday Friday
NATASHA	Wednesday Thursday Friday
RONNIE	Sunday Monday Tuesday
NATASHA	Sunday Monday Tuesday
RONNIE	Wednesday Thursday Friday
NATASHA	Wednesday Thursday Friday
RONNIE	Wednesday Thursday Friday Saturday
NATASHA	Wednesday Thursday Friday Saturday
RONNIE	Thursday Friday Saturday Sunday
NATASHA	Thursday Friday Saturday Sunday
RONNIE	Sunday Monday Tuesday Wednesday Thursday Friday Saturday
NATASHA	Sunday Monday Tuesday Wednesday Thursday Friday Saturday
RONNIE	Monday Tuesday Wednesday Thursday Friday Saturday Sunday
NATASHA	Monday Tuesday Wednesday Thursday Friday Saturday Sunday
RONNIE	Monday Tuesday Wednesday Thursday Friday Saturday Sunday
NATASHA	Monday Tuesday Wednesday Friday Sunday Saturday
RONNIE	you missed out Thursday and you reversed Saturday and Sunday

Natasha doubles up, falls off her chair, rolls over on the floor, gurgling, splurtling, then climbs back

RONNIE	Sunday Monday Tuesday Wednesday Thursday Friday Saturday
NATASHA	Monday Tuesday Friday Sunday
RONNIE	you missed out Sunday at the beginning, Wednesday and Thursday in the middle, replaced Saturday by Sunday at the end

Natasha again creases up into helpless gurgles and splurtles, falls on the floor, rolls over and over, and clambers up again for more

	Monday Tuesday Wednesday Thursday Friday Saturday Sunday
NATASHA	Monday Tuesday Wednesday Thursday Saturday Friday Sunday Monday
RONNIE	you reversed Friday and Saturday and put in Monday

Repeat performance

NATASHA	more, daddy, more
DADDY	that *tickles* you, doesn't it? it tickles the back of your brain
NATASHA	yes (*gurgling and chorkling*) yes daddy, it does. Tickle me daddy

So I did

112

Night

NATASHA	where does the snow dance?
DADDY	I don't know
NATASHA	at the snow ball

113

SUNDAY   *20 June 1976*

NATASHA	Daddy, I've played the piano all the way down

She had started at what we call the bottom left and played her way to the top right

114

27 June 1976

Natasha is reading in silence

NATASHA	can you hear me read?
JUTTA	no, Natasha

115

June 1976

NATASHA	Can God kill himself?
MUMMY	I don't know

116

Monty is an old friend of mine. Natasha hasn't met him before

NATASHA	who gets up in the morning and goes to the shop?
MONTY	I don't know
NATASHA	the shopkeeper

.   .   .

I told Monty that Jutta had told me that Natasha had asked her "Can God kill himself?"

MONTY	there is an incredibly close relationship between sex and death. I will tell you what the question is saying. She is asking "Does God masturbate?"
RONNIE	and that is "Does daddy masturbate?"
MONTY	precisely. She wishes to know whether you do it without mummy, whether you need mummy: whether she can do it with you instead of mummy
RONNIE	there you go
MONTY	I hope you don't mind me being so direct
RONNIE	O not at all

117

A few days ago

ADAM	have you heard this one?
DADDY	which one?
ADAM	this one
DADDY	which one?
ADAM	*this* one
DADDY	aw come on
ADAM	well there was this man see
DADDY	yes
ADAM	now don't interrupt and when he was a boy his father asked him what he wanted and he asked his father to give him a brain so his father gave him a television set and then he grew up a bit and he became a teenager and his father asked him what he wanted and he asked his father to give him a brain so his father gave him a house then he grew up and became a man and his father again asked him what he wanted and he cried "Father! will you give me a brain!" so his father gave him a car and he was driving the car and had an accident, lost most of his brains with brain damage and he was in the ambulance being taken to hospital, with his brain damage you see, and his father was sitting beside him and he said to his father: "Father you should have given me a brain."
DADDY	I don't know whether I think that's funny or not
NATASHA	I think it's funny
DADDY	O well then

118

8 July 1976

One of Adam's friends stayed the night last night

ADAM	kiss David good night, mummy
DAVID	(*aged eight*)
	Oh I'm sorry I only allow myself
	to be kissed by my mummy and other
	relatives

119

MONDAY   *26 July 1976*

ADAM   have you ever been to the *core* of the
            earth?
DADDY   no
ADAM   why not? No one's been there.
            It's very hot and very deep
NATASHA   deeper than this table

      .   .   .

ADAM   they said on TV that the Xmas holiday was
            going to be longer this year
DADDY   yes
ADAM   how can it be longer?
            does it mean it's going to be longer *till*
            Xmas?
DADDY   they can make the Xmas holiday longer, but
            they can't make it longer *till* Xmas

NATASHA	and what is "swearing?"
RONNIE	some words refer to God and divine things. If they are used trivially, or mixed up with nasty words, that's swearing
NATASHA	what does "refer to" mean?
RONNIE	the word table refers to an actual table
NATASHA	oh yes (*impatiently*) and what does "trivial" mean
RONNIE	unimportant
NATASHA	daddy?
RONNIE	yes
NATASHA	daddy, what's the opposite of near?
RONNIE	far
NATASHA	and what's the opposite of queen?
RONNIE	king
NATASHA	and what's the opposite of heaven?
RONNIE	hell
NATASHA	and say them one after the other
RONNIE	how do you mean?
NATASHA	say the opposite of near
RONNIE	far
NATASHA	and the opposite of
RONNIE	yes, ok. far king hell
NATASHA	you swore daddy
RONNIE	yes
NATASHA	you said farking hell daddy! you swore daddy!

DADDY	have you seen a box of matches
NATASHA	yes there's one on the dresser

I go to the dresser. Natasha goes with me. I wonder why.
I find the box of matches, take one out, strike it, and light a cigarette. She is watching me all the time

NATASHA	(*nonplussed*)
	but Adam said they're the pretend matches
DADDY	well this one's lit
NATASHA	can I have a go?

She takes the box, takes a match out of it, strikes it. It lights

NATASHA	but these are the *pretend* matches
DADDY	that's what Adam said
NATASHA	but they *are* the pretend matches
DADDY	Adam must have made a mistake
NATASHA	but *I* put them there
DADDY	well?
NATASHA	can I try another?
DADDY	No. They're not very many. I don't want them all used up
NATASHA	O can I try another?
DADDY	well, ok

She tries another. It lights also

NATASHA	some are pretend matches and some are real
DADDY	I bet you they're all real
NATASHA	I put them *exactly* there
DADDY	Adam must have changed the matches
NATASHA	No. No one could have changed them.
	(*pause*) Oh Daddy! (*in extreme vexation*)
	(*pause*) The matches must have changed

122

31 August 1976

NATASHA   (*to Paul, her grown-up half brother*)
           Could you make your mummy laugh when
           you were a child?

·   ·   ·

ADAM   why did the skeleton not jump over the
           cliff?
ME   I don't know
ADAM   'cos he didn't have any guts

123

CORFU*   *2 September 1976*

The wind is moving the clouds and shaking the branches

NATASHA   is the moon shaking?

·   ·   ·

Nina is younger than Adam and spells very well

NINA   can you spell well?
ADAM   I can spell better than you and you
           can even spell better than me

* We spent the month of September 1976 in Corfu, living together with friends
Arthur and Janette, and their children, Kira (aged 8) and Nina (aged 7).

124

NATASHA	what's the first thing you put in a garden?
ARTHUR	I don't know
NATASHA	your foot

.　　　.　　　.

NATASHA	I don't want to sleep in my bed tonight
ARTHUR	that's alright with me. You can sleep anywhere as far as I'm concerned
NATASHA	I'm going to sleep with you then
KIRA	so am I
NINA	so am I
ARTHUR	(*laughing*) you can't do that
NATASHA	why not? Janette sleeps with you so why can't I sleep with you or Kira sleep with you or Nina sleep with you
ARTHUR	(*laughing*) I'm just sleeping with Janette
NATASHA	that's not fair Arthur, that's not fair
RONNIE	Anyway. Where do you *want* to sleep?
NATASHA	I want to sleep in his nostril
NINA	I want to sleep in his ear
KIRA	I want to sleep inside daddy's penis

NATASHA   (*holding up a little wheel*)
have you seen Max's invisible car?

EVERYONE   no

NATASHA   it's got invisible doors, invisible
seats, an invisible engine, and
three invisible wheels.
It's—*invisible*!

Fish for lunch

ADAM	(*to me*)
	supposing you were very very very hungry,
	you had no food, and you were going to die
	of starvation, would you eat your wife?
RONNIE	you mean Jutta?
ADAM	yes
RONNIE	not if she were alive. If she were
	completely dead, and I would die if
	there was nothing to eat, I might eat
	her body. I might, I might
ARTHUR	who knows who we're eating now?
RONNIE	would you eat mummy?
ADAM	no I wouldn't eat mummy
JUTTA	would you eat Max?
RONNIE	would you eat me?
ARTHUR	do you know that Buddhist story?
	a couple come to a desert with their
	son. There is nothing to eat. They
	are starving. They have to cross the
	desert. The father offers himself to
	be eaten, and the wife. But they
	decide that the pair of them without
	a child have a chance, but one of them
	with a child has no chance. They can
	always have another child. So they eat
	their son. And the Buddhists say that
	anything we eat, we should eat as
	though it's one's own child
RONNIE	or one's grannie. This fish could be
	my grannie
JANETTE	do you recognize her by the smell?

RONNIE   my grannie always dreamed of swimming in
              the Mediterranean, so she reincarnated as a
              fish and was happy just swimming around as
              she had always dreamed of when she was caught
              and now we're eating her
ADAM   (*credulously*)
              did your grannie?
RONNIE   (*interrupting*)
              No I just made it up
JUTTA   this conversation is putting me off my food
ARTHUR   you're the only one it seems to have taken
              this way

127

ADAM   why don't you write a book on
        swearing?

RONNIE a book on swearing?

ADAM   yes. Write a book on what swearing
        means. You know, fuckin' hell, and
        fuckin' this, and fuckin' that, and
        expressions like that. Write a book
        and tell people what that sort of
        thing *means*

128

CORFU   *September 1976*

For days, not a cloud in the sky. Just that Mediterranean sun

ADAM   Do you think the sun is having his
        revenge on the clouds?

129

A few of Adam's questions today, his ninth birthday:

> How is the timing of a hand-grenade regulated?
> Does lead sink in mercury?
> Why does even a grain of sand sink in water?
> Why does even one drop of water fall through
> the air?

and,

> Why does a bazooka tremble?

.   .   .

Natasha tells me that she's never had a nightmare

130

Adam eats breakfast as much standing or jumping up and down as sitting.

How many times has he been told to say please and thank you and pass back what has been passed to him and to look where the honey or the jam or the butter is before calling out for it

and,

ARTHUR   look at me when you ask for something
              Adam

and,

JUTTA   eat with your mouth empty
ADAM   eat with.my mouth empty!
RONNIE   he got you this time
ADAM   ho ho ho
RONNIE   anyway it's obvious what she meant
ADAM   speak with your mouth shut

              .   .   .

NATASHA   Ronnie, I mean, Daddy
DADDY   yes Natasha
NATASHA   how many years till my birthday?
DADDY   but Natasha, I've told you, from one
              birthday to the next is one year, so it's
              always less than a year till your next
              birthday

131

September 1976

In a dispute over a toy

NATASHA   he gave it to me
ADAM   *he* gave it to *you*, and
           I gave it to *me*

September 1976

After dinner

The stars are out. We're all off to make a fire on the beach, Arthur leading the way

NATASHA	Daddy!? Will you give me a carry?
DADDY	Yes, Natasha

And I hoist her up on my shoulders. For how long shall I still be able to do that?

NATASHA	but don't crackle my toes
DADDY	alright Natasha
NATASHA	Arthur's crackled them already

Ah! Now I'm no longer the only one who is allowed to crackle her toes

.   .   .

Night

We are lying on our backs surveying the stars

DADDY	how did all this come about?
ADAM	do you mean "who made it"?
DADDY	well not exactly, but alright
ADAM	a dead man
DADDY	a dead man?! how do you mean?
ADAM	yes. A dead human being

133

14 September 1976

At breakfast

DADDY	what did you mean by a dead human being? A ghost?
ADAM	a ghost, a spirit
DADDY	a spirit
ADAM	yes when you die. One spirit goes up (*indicating from the top of his head*) and another goes down—the good one goes up and the bad one goes down
DADDY	and they are both in us while we are alive?
ADAM	yes
DADDY	and how do you mean a spirit made all this?
ADAM	no I don't really mean a spirit made all *this*
DADDY	the stars?
ADAM	the stars were there before we were. Some people say God made it. God's a spirit. But I don't think God made it. Do you think God exists Arthur?
ARTHUR	yes I think God exists
ADAM	God must have been born
DADDY	how could God be born? If he exists, he must be always, forever
ADAM	how did God walk on the earth then? and anyway who made God?
KIRA	(*to Arthur*) mummy and you made me
ARTHUR	we didn't *make* you
KIRA	where did I come from then?

NINA   people came from people. And God made
the first people

ADAM   People come from creatures who were like
monkeys. They had smaller brains. And they
came from other creatures. Before they
were them there were dinosaurs and things
like that, and fishes and the sea. This
planet is like the stars. It comes from
gases. And then things began to grow and
some grew into people. And they developed
science and technology, from iron and
metals, and made things like we have now,
knives and razor blades, and telephones and
typewriters, and cars and airplanes and
telescopes and things like that—
they developed science and technology,
that's how we find out things, by science

134

During supper

ADAM	Come on, come on
DADDY	how do you mean "Come on, come on"?
ADAM	Come on, come on. Swear! Swear! Let me hear you swearing.
DADDY	Come on, come on yourself. I don't feel like swearing. Why do you want to hear me swearing?
ADAM	I want you to swear
DADDY	I don't want to swear
ADAM	swear! go on swear!
DADDY	I don't feel like swearing
ADAM	swear!
DADDY	why?
ADAM	I want to join you
DADDY	you want to join me?
ADAM	yes I want to join you
DADDY	why do you want to join me?
ADAM	in order to get you out of it
DADDY	in order to get me out of it?
ADAM	yes, in order to get you out of it (*pause*)
DADDY	that's one reason I started it
ADAM	Oh
DADDY	Oh yes. That was one reason. I joined them in order to get them out of it. And then I got into the habit myself
ADAM	oh (*pause*)
DADDY	but I don't feel like it anymore
ADAM	Oh no?
DADDY	no

ADAM	no?
DADDY	is that alright then?
ADAM	that's alright then
DADDY	ok?
ADAM	ok

Corfu   *September 1976*

Afternoon. On the beach

Adam sights an unidentified object floating fairly far out to sea. He proposes a "project" with "component operations." Basically, he, Arthur, and I are to swim out to it, identify it, and if "feasible," bring it ashore.

The first "component operation" passes uneventfully. Arthur, he, and I stand on an offshore rock. Each throws his goggles and snorkle into the sea, dives in after them, retrieves them, puts them on.

Operation Two is to swim out to unidentified floating object. We set off together. Soon Adam and Arthur were drawing ahead of me, and it was not long before I had swum further out than I had done for at least twenty-five years. Further was too far. The object, a black shape, looked just as far away as it had done from the shore. Adam and Arthur seemed thirty or forty feet further out. Then Arthur stopt. Adam was still for going on, but Arthur ordered him back. They swam back together to where I was and the three of us swam back to shore together.

I was grateful to feel the sand under my wobbling knees and very glad to sink back into the safe sand. Arthur looked quite relieved. Adam was livid. I've never seen him so enraged. He was *hopping* mad. He threw himself on the sand, and squirmed and twitched around like an eel with vexation.

He blamed it all on Arthur, for turning back.

Arthur	Don't blame me! It was *way* off
Adam	No it wasn't
Jutta	(*who had been watching from the shore*) You were only halfway there
Adam	No we weren't. We were almost there
Daddy	No we were not almost there. It was still *far* away. Definitely *too* far away
Adam	It wasn't

DADDY	It was
ARTHUR	Adam! (*he wasn't listening*) Adam!! Your mummy saw it from the shore
ADAM	she did not
DADDY	It was too far

Adam looked at us all

DADDY	I'm telling you. It was too far
ARTHUR	It was still far away
JUTTA	You weren't even halfway there

He was completely surrounded

ADAM	You're all lying
ARTHUR	Look. Why should we lie to you Adam. We're all friends

Adam said nothing

ARTHUR	It was too far for me, and it was definitely too far for you

He still said nothing

DADDY	Look. You still can't swim further than Arthur, or me, even
ADAM	How do you know?
DADDY	Your mummy saw us from the shore We were only halfway there
JUTTA	that's right
ADAM	she's lying
JUTTA	No I'm not. You won't listen to anyone that's your trouble
ADAM	well I'm not going to listen to you
JUTTA	You'd better watch it. You had better watch it
DADDY	Do you seriously think that you know better than everyone else

Adam said nothing
We all took a short breather. Except Adam, who was still "at it,"
though he was silent

DADDY   Anyway. It's not a defeat
ADAM   Yes it is

And it all started up again. After the third full round of the above,
with minor variations, Adam's vehemence had in no way abated

JUTTA   it was an optical illusion
ADAM   a what??
JUTTA   an optical illusion
ADAM   An optical illusion!? What is an
              "optical illusion"?
JUTTA   something that looks different from what
              it is
ADAM   you mean I can't believe my eyes?!
DADDY   Well. Not always. Not just like that. Not
              without reservations
ADAM   reservations!?

It went on and on

136

Evening

ADAM	if you had a wish what would it be?
ME	can it be for a state or a thing or . . .
ADAM	anything you like
ME	I would like to be happy—if I was *happy* then a lot of things would have to be right
ADAM	and what would your next wish be?
ME	that everyone else be happy
ADAM	*everyone*? in the whole world?
ME	yes. why not?
ADAM	even against their will?
JUTTA	do you think there's anyone who doesn't want to be happy?
ME	well ok. I don't want to *force* anyone to be happy. Let's say all those who want to be happy can be happy (*pause*)
ADAM	daddy?
DADDY	yes
ADAM	would you rather be strong or weak?
DADDY	I would rather be strong
ADAM	would you rather be wise or stupid?
DADDY	I would rather be wise
ADAM	would you rather be weak and wise, or stupid and strong?
DADDY	weak and wise
ADAM	and would you rather be happy and weak, or proud and strong
DADDY	happy and weak

137

NATASHA   Did you write this book?*
DADDY   yes
NATASHA   they've printed it very well (*turning the pages*)
                  there's not much on the paper. Look, there's
                  hardly anything on that page. Or that page.
                  There's the littlest *I've* ever seen. I think
                  this is the *silliest* book I've ever seen

* *Do You Love Me?*

ADAM	daddy?
DADDY	yes Adam
ADAM	when's my birthday?
DADDY	don't you know your birthday by now?
ADAM	yes but how long is it till my birthday?
DADDY	how do you mean?
ADAM	how many months?
DADDY	don't you know the months of the year yet?
ADAM	O come on daddy
DADDY	well this is October. Then it'll be November, December, January, February, March, April, May, June, July, August, *September*
ADAM	Oh my God
DADDY	well there's no hurry
JUTTA	everyone's got a birthday before you except daddy
ADAM	Oh (*petulantly*)
DADDY	don't you know that yet? anyway I'm in no hurry for my next birthday
ADAM	*I'm* in a hurry
DADDY	you'll never be nine again
ADAM	I don't want to be
DADDY	Your next birthday you'll be ten
ADAM	I know. I can't wait
DADDY	you should make the most of every day in your life Every minute you'll never have a second over again
ADAM	would you like to be young again? would you like to be nine again? would you like to be eighteen again? come on answer. Would you like to be twenty-eight again?
DADDY	would I like my life over again?

139

ADAM   daddy, will you teach me a Christmas
carol, in a *smart* key

140

THURSDAY   *30 December 1976*

Night

Jutta, Adam, Natasha, and Max have just returned from Stuttgart
after a week with Opa and Omilie, and the rest of Jutta's family.
I came back home a few days earlier.

Now, Natasha and I are sitting snugly on the sofa, snow and frost
outside

NATASHA   were you playing the piano when we rang
the bell?
DADDY   no
NATASHA   were you watching television?
DADDY   no
NATASHA   were you having something to eat?
DADDY   no
NATASHA   were you writing?
DADDY   no
NATASHA   were you walking up and down?
DADDY   no
NATASHA   were you smoking your pipe?
DADDY   no
NATASHA   were you studying?

DADDY	no
NATASHA	were you just sitting down?!
DADDY	I was just sitting down
NATASHA	Oh, at last I know what you were doing when we rang the bell
DADDY	And I was waiting for you to ring the bell
NATASHA	did you know we were coming?
DADDY	I was expecting you
NATASHA	but did you *know* we were coming?
DADDY	well when *I* got back from Stuttgart it was just twenty past seven, so I was looking at my watch and it was just twenty past seven so I thought I would just sit down and wait for the doorbell to ring
NATASHA	and did you know it was going to ring
DADDY	I thought it would then I heard your voices, and then I knew it would, and it did. Just at twenty-five minutes past seven

A hug

141

Evening in my study

NATASHA (*comes in: offers me some bubble gum*)
I can blow a bubble with this bubble
gum (*pause*) (*reluctantly*) I did it for
the first time this afternoon (*she is not getting
on very well at it now*) Can you blow bubble
gum?

DADDY (*has a go: unsuccessful*) no

NATASHA yes you can. Adam can blow *big* ones.

DADDY well there you are that's something he
can do I can't do

NATASHA you can't blow bubble gum! (*incredulously*)

DADDY when I was your age I wasn't allowed
bubble gum so I never got the practice
(*evidently this is not a sufficient
excuse*) and when I grew up I never felt
in the mood

NATASHA and you're the oldest, and you can't
blow bubble gum!

DADDY well maybe I *could* if I tried, but I've
never put my mind to it

NATASHA (*wandering off, shaking her head*) and
you're the oldest and you can't blow
bubble gum

· · ·

Jutta, Adam, Natasha, and I saw the New Year in together, over a
bottle of champagne

Adam became engrossed with how the cork could have been gotten
into the bottle

"Keep that cork, I want to study it."

142

Natasha has been playing a Haydn air and a melody, on the piano.

She had the idea of playing them together

Thus

I told her she had discovered counterpoint!

But she wasn't interested

143

It's the end of another late-night western

The goodie and the baddie stand facing each other for what can only be the last time

They draw
The badman begins to fall
His eyes turn up. He has a final glimpse of the sun

NATASHA   He said "Do You Love Me?"

He dies

144

March 1977

Jutta is taken aback by coming upon Adam making grandiose magical passes with a stick at our ailing palm tree in the hall

JUTTA   Can I believe my eyes?
                 Can I believe my eyes?
ADAM   No

Later

JUTTA   I couldn't believe my ears!

About the Author

R. D. Laing studied medicine at Glasgow University. He
was a psychiatrist in the British army and a physician at
the Glasgow Royal Mental Hospital, and taught at the
University of Glasgow. Subsequently, he joined the
Tavistock Clinic and was later appointed Director of the
Langham Clinic in London. From 1961 to 1967 he
undertook research into families, and he is now in private
practice as a psychoanalyst.

Since 1964, Dr. Laing has been President of the
Philadelphia Association in London. This organization is
mainly concerned with setting up households as places
of sanctuary, asylum, refuge, and dwelling, where people
may live without receiving any treatment they do not want.

He is the author of numerous articles and reviews. His
other books are *The Divided Self, Self and Others,
Reason and Violence* (with David Cooper), *Sanity,
Madness and the Family,* Vol. 1: *The Families of
Schizophrenics* (with Aaron Esterson), *Interpersonal
Perception: A Theory and a Method of Research* (with
H. Phillipson and A. R. Lee), *The Politics of Experience,
The Politics of the Family, Knots, The Facts of Life,*
and *Do You Love Me?*